★
THE
BIG
TIME

IGGY AZALEA

LAURA K. MURRAY

CREATIVE EDUCATION

IGGY AZALEA

TABLE OF CONTENTS

MEET IGGY

ggy stands on a stage. The music begins to thump. Iggy takes a deep breath and lifts her microphone. She starts speaking so fast! Some of her words **rhyme**. The crowd claps and cheers!

ggy Azalea is an Australian rapper. Her real name is Amethyst Kelly. Many people think she is one of the best rappers today. Fans love her wild outfits and clever **lyrics** (*LEER-icks*).

....

Iggy writes songs under her real name.

IGGY'S CHILDHOOD

Amethyst was born June 7, 1990. She grew up in New South Wales, Australia. Her family lived on Azalea Street. She had a dog named Iggy! In school, Amethyst liked art. But she had a hard time making friends.

Iggy has fun when she goes back to visit Australia.

NEW SOUTH WALES, AUSTRALIA

GETTING INTO RAP

Amethyst loved *hip-hop* music. She started rapping at age 14. Then she left high school early. At age 16, she moved to the United States alone. She started calling herself Iggy Azalea.

··

Iggy knew only one person in the U.S. when she moved there.

ggy moved to different cities. She worked and saved money. There were not many female rappers. But Iggy kept rapping. By 2012, millions of people watched her videos online. Iggy wanted to make an album.

. . . .

Iggy started teaming up with other artists.

THE BIG TIME

In 2012, a magazine listed Iggy as a top new rapper. More people started listening to her music. Iggy's first album, *The New Classic*, came out in 2014. It had the hit song "Fancy," with Charli XCX. Iggy also rapped on Ariana Grande's song "Problem."

. . . .

The New Classic *won best rap album at the 2014 American Music Awards.*

ggy won Teen Choice Awards and other honors for her music and videos. She worked as a model, too. She even hosted a TV show about *fashion*. Iggy became known for her bright, bold clothes!

. . . .

Iggy paired up with singer Jennifer Hudson for a 2015 performance.

OFF THE STAGE

When Iggy is not rapping, she hangs out with friends. She cooks and relaxes. She likes riding roller coasters and playing tennis. She goes to fashion shows, too.

Iggy's fans like to see what she will wear for fashion shows.

WHAT IS NEXT?

ggy canceled her Great Escape Tour in 2015. But she was hard at work on her next album. Iggy is sure to keep fans excited for years to come!

Iggy was named top rap artist at the 2015 Billboard Music Awards.

WHAT IGGY SAYS ABOUT ...

MOVING TO THE U.S.

"It was about going somewhere to feel like I could fit in."

THE SUCCESS OF "FANCY"

"I went from having nothing to having everything I could possibly want. It's weird."

UNUSUAL MUSIC VIDEOS

"I always loved the videos that were a bit out of the box ... if it has a flying horse, I'm interested."

GLOSSARY

fashion a certain style or way of dressing

hip-hop a style of music that has rap in it

lyrics the words to a song

rhyme to have the same ending sound, like "cat" and "hat"

WEBSITES

Iggy Azalea
http://iggyazalea.com/
This is Iggy's own website, with news, videos, and more.

Iggy Azalea Profile
http://www.billboard.com/artist/5694588/iggy-azalea
See photos, news, and music overviews about Iggy.

READ MORE

Frisch, Aaron. *Lady Gaga*. Mankato, Minn.: Creative Education, 2013.

Murray, Laura K. *Ariana Grande*. Mankato, Minn.: Creative Education, 2017.

INDEX

PUBLISHED BY Creative Education
P.O. Box 227, Mankato, Minnesota 56002
Creative Education is an imprint of The Creative Company
www.thecreativecompany.us

DESIGN AND PRODUCTION BY Christine Vanderbeek
ART DIRECTION BY Rita Marshall
PRINTED IN the United States of America

PHOTOGRAPHS BY Alamy (WENN Ltd), Corbis (MARIO ANZUONI/ Reuters, Sayre Berman, Gilbert Carrasquillo/Splash News, John Davidson, GoldenEye/London Entertainment/Splash News, Grey Wasp/Splash News, Amy Harris, Paul A. Hebert/Press Line Photos, Michael Hurcomb, Oraito/Splash News, PG/Splash News, Retna Ltd., Splash News/Splash News), iStockphoto (colevineyard), Shutterstock (ekler)

LIBRARY OF CONGRESS CATALOGING-IN-PUBLICATION DATA
Murray, Laura K.
Iggy Azalea / Laura K. Murray.
p. cm. — (The big time)
Includes index.
Summary: An elementary introduction to the life, work, and popularity of Iggy Azalea, an Australian rapper who became known for her fast rhymes and gained fame with such hit songs as "Fancy."

ISBN 978-1-60818-671-6 (HARDCOVER)
ISBN 978-1-56660-707-0 (EBOOK)
1. Azalea, Iggy, 1990–. 2. Rap musicians—Biography. I. Title.
ML420.A95M87 2016
782.421649092—dc23 [B] 2015026256

CCSS: RI.1.1, 2, 3, 4, 5, 6, 7; RI.2.1, 2, 5, 6, 7; RI.3.1, 5, 7, 8; RI.4.3, 5; RF.1.1, 3, 4; RF.2.3, 4

FIRST EDITION 9 8 7 6 5 4 3 2 1